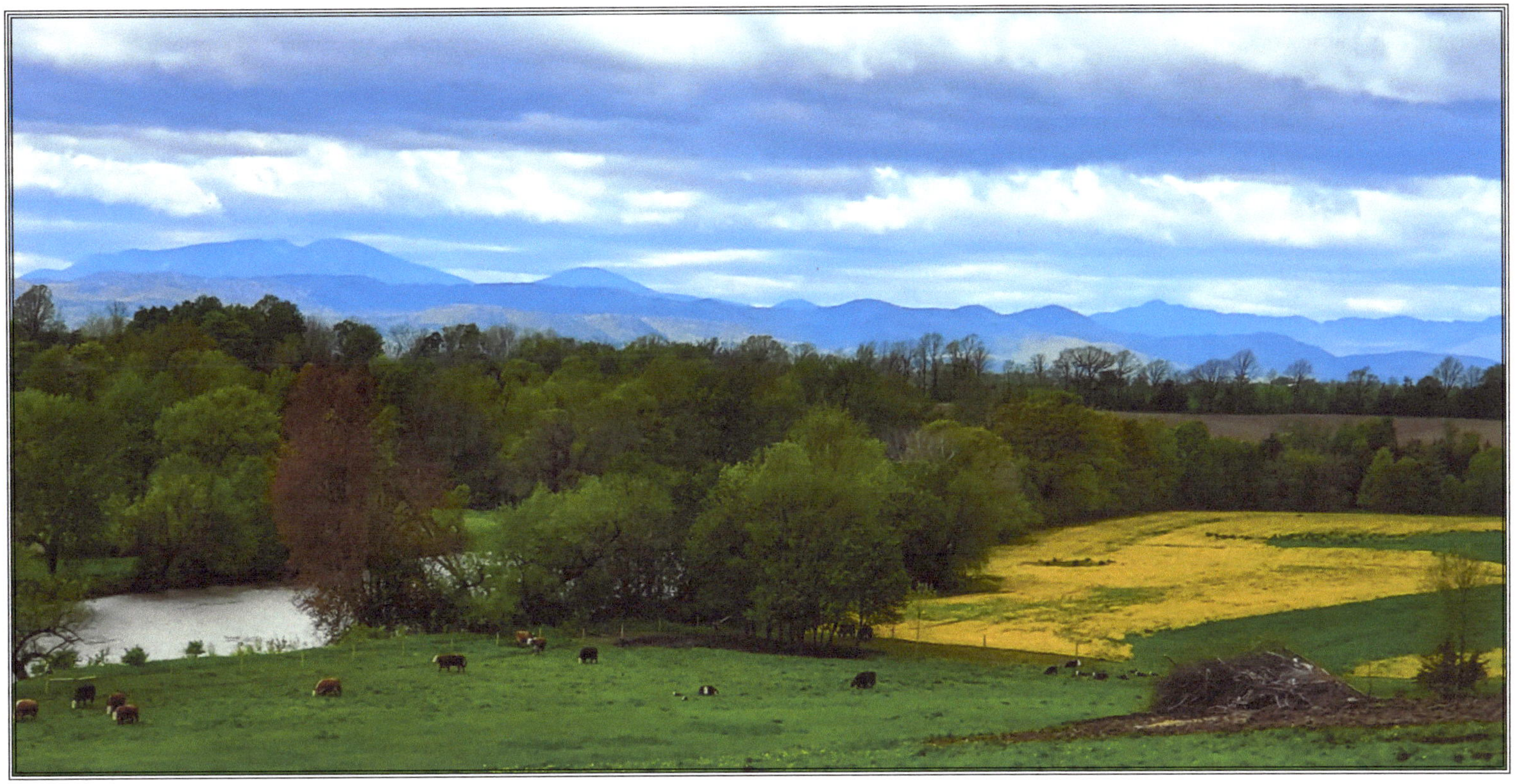

New England Ramblings

Seeking spiritual revival in a land of beauty

–J. James Mancuso

Albertville, Alabama, USA

Copyright © 2020-2021 J. James Mancuso
Cover and Interior Design © 2020-2021 Warner House Press
All rights reserved. No part of this publication may be reproduced, stored in a retrieval system, or transmitted in any form or any means, electronic, or print, without the written permission of the publisher. The only exceptions are brief quotations in written reviews and scholarly works.
All photographs are the original work of J. James Mancuso.

Scripture quotations from The Holy Bible, English Standard Version®,
copyright © 2001 by Crossway Bibles, a publishing ministry of Good News Publishers.
Used by permission. All rights reserved.

For more information, contact:
Warner House Press
1325 Lane Switch Road
Albertville, Alabama 35951
https://warner.house

Published 2020
Printed in the United States of America

26 25 24 23 22 21 2 3 4 5

ISBN: 978-1-951890-25-4

Library of Congress Cataloging-in-Publication Data

Mancuso, J. James, 1958-
   New England Ramblings: seeking spiritual revival in a land of beauty / J. James Mancuso
   Albertville, AL: Warner House Press, 2021, rev. ed.
   ii, 52 pages : color photographs; 23 cm.
   ISBN 978-1-951890-25-4
1. Devotionals—New England 2. Revival—New England 3. New England—picture books.
BV4811 .M324 2021

By Way of Introduction

New England Ramblings invites you to—

- *ramble through back roads on a journey, enjoying picturesque New England–seeing some of its scenery and fine architecture*
- *ramble through the seasons of the year, delighting in the changing vistas–experiencing the variety of nature*
- *ramble through the spiritual journey of living out faith in Christ–pondering poetry and devotional observations*

But most important, New England Ramblings is a plea for prayer for the souls of men and women walking in spiritual darkness. It is an urgent call for Christians to pray for a powerful spiritual revival in this region.

Many people associate New England with beautiful old white churches with tall steeples. Students of theological history soon learn that much of America's bedrock of faith—especially faith expressed in the American concepts of liberty and religious freedom—was birthed in the cradle of New England. Surely, nearly every educated American has learned of the role of this region in the founding of America and the establishment of Christendom in our country.

New England comprises six states: Maine, New Hampshire, Vermont, Massachusetts, Rhode Island, and Connecticut. Historically, this area has been home to great revivals led by famous preachers and evangelists such as Jonathan Edwards, George Whitefield, and Dwight L. Moody. But what is the current spiritual state of this beautiful region? Sadly, it is no longer a land where a large portion of the population is made up of evangelical, Bible-believing Christians.

How great is the darkness here? How extensive is the lostness? In 2005, Barna Research found that one out of six residents of Massachusetts and Connecticut is either atheist or agnostic—that's twice the national average. Hartford, Connecticut, Providence, Rhode Island, and nearby Albany, New York, rank as the most post-Christian, least Bible-oriented metropolitan areas in the country. In many parts of New England, only one or two percent of the population attends any church at all. In some of its pulpits, the truth of the life-changing gospel has been exchanged for heresy and New Age philosophy.

At this point in time, the current residents of the six states rarely ever hear a clear presentation of the gospel—the simple good news that salvation is offered freely to anyone who repents of sin and takes God's only son, Jesus Christ, as savior and Lord.

In many important ways, Massachusetts was home to great movements that have shaped American Christianity. Historically, this state was the cradle of American Christian culture and the launching ground of great revivals.

The pilgrims of Plymouth Plantation, and other Puritan settlers in the early 1600s, established a colony based on religious freedom and set forth a Christian worldview that gave birth to our concepts of liberty and democracy.

Jonathan Edwards, pastor of the church in Northampton, preached the world-famous sermon "Sinners in the Hands of an Angry God" in Enfield, Connecticut in 1741. He was used mightily of God to lead many to faith and to produce other great sermons and significant Christian literature. The entire American foreign missions movement owes its humble beginnings to a group of five young Christian college students in Williamstown who had a burden to reach the lost. Beginning with their pioneering efforts in 1812, missions agencies have sent thousands of trained missionaries around the globe to bring the good news of the gospel to untold millions.

Renowned evangelist Dwight L. Moody, who brought the gospel to a million people worldwide from 1873 to 1899, hailed from Northfield.

But today—by sad contrast—Massachusetts has the lowest percentage of evangelical Christians of the densely populated states.

So, the need for reaching the population of New England with the gospel is great. More than ever, New England needs light to dispel its spiritual darkness. This region is poised for yet another great awakening.

As you look through New England Ramblings, enjoy the beauty of the region. See what a lovely place gave birth to American Christianity. Ponder how the Lord speaks through His creation and calls us to repentance and a right relationship with Him through His Son. But, above all, pray that the Lord would once again do a mighty work in this region. Pray for the churches of New England. Pray that the Lord would bless them with another great revival.

First Baptist Church, Providence, Rhode Island

New England Throughout the Year

Winter will not weary of his wild whitening ways.
Each of his sad victims wonders daily why he stays.

Spring delays her entrance like a naughty, dawdling child.
O, that she would bless us with her touch so warm and mild.

Summer runs too quickly as we relish her delights:
Gentle breezes, forest hikes, and softly starlit nights.

Autumn harvests cheer us: cider doughnuts, pumpkins round.
Swaying maple trees with red and orange leaves abound.

Thoughts on the New Year

Before us yawns the new year: a long stretch of unknown highway that will sometimes take us where we do not want to go and provide many bumps and sharp turns. But it will also carry us through pleasant meadows, over mountain peaks, and past valley streams. Dear Lord, walk with me every mile, and carry me when I need it.

As we clean out our homes from the revelries of Christmas, we sweep dead pine needles over the thresholds and greet a new beginning. Yet… in the empty silence devoid of candles and Christmas trees, the Lord gives us a new yearning for His kingdom.

We pray that this year, O Lord, the long-awaited revival that our region needs so desperately will begin in earnest. We have learned about the Great Awakenings of the 18th and 19th centuries, and we remember how evangelists like Billy Graham stirred hearts in the 20th. But now this corner of the country, once the cradle of American Christianity, has grown cold to the gospel, ignorant of its heritage, deaf to truth, and blind to the emptiness of life in a postmodern, post-Christian society.

We yearn for revival, Lord. Let it be this year.

God sends a colorful sunset to linger on in our minds throughout the dark night.

Interior of First Baptist Church, Providence, Rhode Island

O LORD, I have heard the report of you,
and your work, O LORD, do I fear.
In the midst of the years revive it;
in the midst of the years make it known;
in wrath remember mercy. (Habakkuk 3:2)

Even at times when things seem dark and dead, God is at work.

Gray Dawn

When God took up to paint this dawn,
A chilling, dismal winter's day,
Alas, His palette was constrained
To gray, just gray, just shades of gray.

Gray skies, gray clouds, gray roads, gray trees,
An ever-widening spread of gray.
The wash of color elsewhere lies
This cold and lifeless winter's day.

Hard edges frame a picture 'round
To point our eyes to brilliant views.
This morning stands to contrast with
The dazzling wash of summer's hues.

He who has an ear, let him hear what the Spirit says to the churches.
(Revelation 3:22)

Better Prepared

Statements carved into some of these gravestones still proclaim the sure hope that these early settlers had placed in the power of the resurrection of their risen Lord.

During the icy winter, New Englanders know one thing about positioning their cars: they park facing out. Savvy drivers realize that often one cannot be sure just how icy or slushy the parking space will be when one returns to his car. So, the safest thing to do, especially on a hill, is to park facing out: one can always slip the car in neutral and let it slide forward.

As believers, this is our approach to life on earth. All that we ought to be doing and saying should be inspired by our knowledge of eternity. We are aiming our earthly lives at heaven. We are orienting ourselves toward our maker and savior, not conforming to our surroundings. Earth is not our home forever, so we choose how we spend our time here based on heavenly reward.

We park facing out.

Weary Vermonters do not welcome March snowfalls, though they admit they are often the loveliest.

When the humble see it, they will be glad.
You who seek God–let your hearts revive. (Psalm 69:32)

Fresh Linen Snowfall

God spread new linen on a winter's night;
All of His linen was just white on white.
Cold, crisp, and sparkling, shiny, and bright–
All for His glory and children's delight.

Old First Church, white on white. Unto the eyes a classic delight.

The "chocolate mousse" holds snowy-white cream in his horns.

What can look grim and lifeless one day will someday be green and lively.

But you are a chosen race, a royal priesthood, a holy nation, a people for his own possession,
that you may proclaim the excellencies of him who called you out of darkness into his marvel-
ous light. (1 Peter 2:9)

Late March

When we rise on the first day of spring to find a cold, icy extension of winter, we talk of the "hope" of spring. It is a surety, a promise—a gift given, but as yet unrealized. We have this sure promise and we cling to it as we trudge wearily over cold, ugly slush and melting snow. But the power of spring will come, and all will be made anew, and we will live in the full joy of life. Of that fact, we are positively certain.

It is no coincidence that Christ's resurrection occurred in spring. Like the hope of spring, it is a gift of glory for us, promised, but not yet fully realized.

Just as the new spring revives a weary land, so too will be the resurrection for all those found in Christ when we fully realize the joy of The Ultimate Spring.

Restore to me the joy of your salvation,
and uphold me with a willing spirit.
Then I will teach transgressors your ways,
and sinners will return to you. (Psalm 51:12–13)

Pray for the pastors of small rural churches and the people they minister to.

Long ago, this old inn once welcomed weary travelers.

Furnaces

The first really warm days arrive in early spring. We shed our coats and melancholy moods and embrace the world around us that has decided to not be hostile. And we turn off the furnace. Well, for now. We know that, in New England, one warm day in late March or early April does not a summer make. We know we'll need the life-giving warmth of that furnace again in a few days, and now and then on chilly nights well into May too. And maybe after that once or twice. Of course, we would never dream of getting rid of our furnaces in summer—we service them and get them ready for use again in the autumn. We know we'll need them again because we know that homes without heat are useless.

But what about abandoned buildings that have no heat? How do they fare? This inn, once a beautiful haven for weary travelers, is now a spooky wreck. Without warmth and care for the last 40 years, this inn has decayed into a haven fit only for bats and vermin.

New England needs the gospel. It warms the culture. It has the power to change individual hearts, which then keep families intact and build strong communities. God's Word is true and dependable. It shows us how to live and be assured of eternal salvation. We need its warm touch in our lives constantly, like we need furnaces.

Spiritually, New England has grown dark and cold. Its residents shut down the furnace of God's love and truth a long time ago.

We need to ignite that flame again. We are praying fervently for New England to return to its roots. Long ago this was the cradle of American Christianity, and it needs to be again.

Lord, help faithful pastors show New England how to turn the furnace back on.

The Green Mountains form a handsome backdrop to fields and forests on a spring day.

Which Part Lasts Forever?

When a New England man buys a new machine, he immediately wants to know which parts he will need to replace soon and which will last beyond his lifetime. The big problem in this region, nowadays, is that these same people who apply that good sense and prudent stewardship to their possessions are not geared to thinking that way about themselves—that is, about body and soul. The soul lasts forever; the body does not.

All the focus of daily life is on the temporal, not the eternal. Most people in this region today spend all their time working for what they cannot keep beyond the grave, worrying about status and appearance, and worshiping what is fleeting. So, we ought to be very interested indeed in what renews our inner self—what builds up our soul.

The faithful Christians that settled New England had no such vain imagination. They knew that the body must be cared for and nourished, but that the soul would live for an eternity—in glory or in torment. They placed the greater emphasis of Christian living squarely on what matters: that the inner self would be renewed day by day through things like prayer, Bible study, worship, and acts of mercy. Through these joyous activities, a believer lays up treasure in Heaven, feeds the soul, builds up the kingdom, benefits others, and gives God the glory.

Each day, the outer self deteriorates a little more. Over time, the effect is obvious.

So do not lose heart.
Though our outer self is deteriorating, still our inner self is being renewed day by day.
(2 Corinthians 4:16)

Spring's Good News

Sunshine lights up a spring day in Chester, Vermont.

But the angel said to the women, "Do not be afraid, for I know that you seek Jesus who was crucified. He's not here, for he has risen, as he said. Come, see the place where the Lord was lying. Then go quickly and tell his disciples that He has risen from the dead." (Matthew 28:6–7)

What other news has captivated the hearts and souls of sinful man to a greater degree than this? What could? These are words that changed not only the entire course of human history, but the very understanding of who God is, how much He loves us, and what He has sacrificed on our behalf. This news requires a personal response.

He is risen.

He is risen indeed.

But when the goodness and loving kindness of God our Savior appeared, he saved us, not because of works done by us in righteousness, but according to his own mercy, by the washing of regeneration and renewal of the Holy Spirit. (Titus 3:4–5)

Vision

One chilly spring evening a few years ago, I was staying at my buddy Ed's mountain cabin just north of Rutland, Vermont, and was having trouble starting his gas fireplace. I called him and he explained to me, over the phone, exactly how to do it, pointing out precise locations and details as if he were standing in the room next to the fireplace. I followed his instructions easily and fired it up. Ed, who is by calling a pastor, is astoundingly adept at explaining things that are in other places—and which he cannot see but still understands intimately.

On Sunday he preached about heaven.

Scalloped spring clouds form a handsome sky above a church in Chester, Vermont.

Ginko trees are a rare treat; their leaves form an interesting frame.

Early morning on the wharf in Nantucket awaiting the ferry back to Cape Cod.

Restore us, O God of hosts!
Let your face shine, that we may be saved! (Psalm 80:7)

What will Remain?

A restored train station delights visitors to North Bennington.

In the end, only the things we do in concern for one another matter—not our possessions, nor our degrees, though they are necessary and good. If all the world's a stage and we are its hapless actors, then the props are not ours, neither are the sets.

Only the effect we have on the audience remains.

The childhood home of Dwight L. Moody in Northfield, Massachusetts is now a museum.

A park is a place to rest and think and ponder God's truth.

You did not choose me, but I chose you and appointed you that you should go and bear fruit and that your fruit should abide, so that whatever you ask the Father in my name, he may give it to you. (John 15:16)

Sameness and Newness

Each morning the same sun arrives, yet it does so in its own splendor—new each morning—and it heralds a day that cannot be exactly the same as the one before. Expect the Lord to adorn life's constants with new and different accents each time. Feel secure in the sameness; take delight in the new.

The steadfast love of the LORD never ceases.
His mercies never come to an end; they are new every morning.
(Lamentations 3:22–23)

A modern replica of a crude frontier home built by pioneers seeking religious freedom.

The Collinsville Congregational Church (Connecticut) was blessed greatly during the second Great Awakening.

At sunset, the Lord flings a splendor of color to delight our eyes.

Two Hands

These days, in New England, one finds two different approaches to life quite prevalent.
Tragically, neither of them results in happiness and contentment.

On the one hand are people who have so little hope that they let go of all the good things in life
and drag themselves through meaningless days in despair.

On the other hand are those who grip life so tightly that, when tragedies take away something or someone they treasure,
they cannot cope with the loss.

A few centuries ago, such was not the case. Most of the pioneers who settled the towns of New England believed unto Christ for salvation and walked humbly before God, trusting Him for their lives and health and safety. And they knew that tragedy and loss were a part of their earthly lives. They faced both with the biblical assurance that, in the end, "all things work together for the good of those who are called according to His purpose." That assurance gave them strength in hard times and prevented greed and over-reliance on self in times of ease.

We all need balance, living our lives with two hands outstretched to divine provision.
With fingers open, we can graciously take into our hands what God designs and desires to give us.
Then, we need to courageously keep from shrinking back and dropping what God has given us to hold onto.
But we also need to never grip our gifts so tightly that we mangle them.

Let us lift up our hearts and hands to God in heaven. (Lamentations 3:41)

Order Matters

New England is an orderly place. Sometimes. At least, it started out that way. Those who settled this area came with a desire that things be done decently and in order, an ethic they derived from 1 Corinthians 14:40. Keeping things in order preserves life; disorderliness ruins it.

Even the order we use when spelling words makes a great difference in saying what we mean and meaning what we write: Satan and Santa have the same letters, but the order is different. They are two beings, one real and one imaginary, with opposite objectives, yet whose names are spelled with the same five letters. Order matters.

God calls us to put Him first in our lives and let all our desires and pursuits be in good order after Him—not necessarily eliminated, just put in order. When we put God first, our lives are filled with joy. Not always pleasure and ease, but an abiding joy.

So, when we ask God to show us how to put the elements of our lives in order, we keep the end in mind. To one, He will say, "Depart from me, you worker of iniquity." To the other, He will say, "Well done, good and faithful servant."

Condemnation and commendation have almost all the same letters, just a little rearranged. In the end, each person receives one or the other.

The Katharine Seymour Day home, which belonged to a relative of Harrie Beecher Stowe and now houses the Stowe research library.

In the Nook Farm enclave of Hartford, Connecticut, one can tour the lavish, fascinating former home of author Mark Twain.

Next to the Twain home, one can also tour the former home of another famous author, Harriet Beecher Stowe.

Museums near this boat harbor in Mystic, Connecticut, offer the chance to experience coastal life of a bygone era.

Summer evenings in York Beach often feature clouds vibrantly lit by the setting sun.

A lone tree greets travelers as they reach the shore of Lake Champlain.

On summer days, Lake Shaftsbury provides a calm, quiet respite from the hectic pace of life.

Who's in Charge?

In turbulent times of unprecedented chaos and loss, no one has a guidebook to show us what to do and how to respond to each new wave of change. As believers, we embrace the times we live in, knowing that our faith is founded on the solid rock who preserves and sustains us, who holds our lived in His hands, who knows the future, and who cares for those who have repented of sin and called on the name of Christ for salvation.

We may not have *a manual*, but we have *Emmanuel*.

A home in Providence, Rhode Island, the city where founder Roger Williams established a colony based on true religious freedom.

This home in South Windsor, Connecticut once belonged to Asahel Nettleton, who brought thousands to faith in Christ through his preaching in New England and New York in the early 1800s.

Beautiful old homes line Benefit Street in Providence, Rhode Island.

If my people who are called by my name humble themselves, and pray and seek my face and turn from their wicked ways, then I will hear from heaven and will forgive their sin and heal their land. (2 Chronicles 7:14)

Spring's blossoms greet the eye, replacing winter's drabness with color.

A playfully creative statue-- this boy's boot fills the fountain at the Wallingford Inn.

This monument commemorates the birthplace of the American foreign missions movement in 1806.

19

Focus

I was trying to photograph my granddaughter while she was making cookies. Each time I told her to look at me and smile, she just kept on doing what she wanted to do and muttering the word "cheese."

At that moment I wondered if this was how God sees us.

He is trying to get us to focus on Him, but we just keep doing what we feel like and muttering some magic word.

The longest name for a lake in America.

All that's left of a once busy mill in Dorset Hollow, Vermont-- a rusting wheel and memories.

Restore us to yourself, O LORD, that we may be restored!
Renew our days as of old. (Lamentations 5:21)

Recycling done Green Mountain style: turning old skis into chairs.

On Revival

Eating at a restaurant in Queechee, Vermont includes a great view of the waterfalls.

We can never say a magic word that will make revival happen again in New England. We need to be looking at the Lord—studying His word, studying His nature, and leaving behind the former passions that once ensnared us.

Or think of the hope for revival this way: When we boast that we have sailed a boat across the open sea, we ought to be humbly declaring that the wind blew it across for us. Still, it is important to point out that had we not set the sails and directed the boat, it would not have crossed the sea. So it is with revival—we cannot move the boat ourselves, but God insists that we set the sail and steer the rudder.

Today we must be about the business of setting sails.

Kayaking on Echo Lake on a warm summer day delights body and soul.

The sea is his, for he made it,
and his hands formed the dry land. (Psalm 95:5)

The Author of Beauty

Few places in North America rival the Maine seacoast for the beauty of its natural crags and wave-drenched rocks shimmering in summer sunlight. Fortunately, the first settlers complemented God's handiwork with fine wooden homes and majestic lighthouses.

The Maine Coast—to see it is to understand that God does want His world to be beautiful.

Visitors to Pemaquid Point Light may tour the interior of the Lighthouse.

Strolling on the Marginal Way, one can see beautiful vistas of the Atlantic.

From inside a lighthouse on Cape Elizabeth, one gains a spectacular view of the Maine coast.

And after you have suffered a little while, the God of all grace, who has called you to his eternal glory in Christ, will himself restore, confirm, strengthen, and establish you.
(I Peter 5:10)

Coastal bogs provide a respite from the hurry-scurry pace of urban life.

The setting sun illuminates the Josiah River as it finally reaches the ocean.

In coastal Maine, morning fog outlines the intricate detail of spider webs.

Painter Thomas Cole often sought to capture moments like this on his canvas.

Lighthouses

Most Americans have seen photographs of the iconic Portland Head Light. It is an astoundingly beautiful lighthouse that I have had the pleasure of visiting several times. Recently, I watched other visitors running up and down trails in the park that surrounds it, taking their own photos from many different vantage points. I heard them exclaim, "Oh, it's even prettier from this angle," as they scampered up the steps. Indeed, they were right; each new angle provides a handsome sight to behold.

I waited for many years for my first chance to go there and see it. That first visit, coming at the end of a long, hot drive on a summer day, disappointed me and my family greatly. Since the whole coast was banked in with dense fog, we were unable to take any stunning photos of this beautiful landmark. The loud foghorn was blasting once a minute.

I expressed my dismay to a native standing nearby.

"Ay-uh," he retorted in the typical, no-nonsense, brusque tone, "can't say as it would be very useful on a sunny day."

Churches are like lighthouses. Yes, they should be beautiful buildings, dedicated to the glory of a God that instills in us a need for beauty.

But they have a job to do—guide people lost in the fog.

"Midnight Blue" at Nubble Light in Cape Neddick, Maine during the fleeting moments of twilight.

A lighthouse might be a beautiful sight to behold on a sunny day, but it saves lives on foggy ones.

Many enjoy boating on New England's coastal waterways.

Crabs hide in tidal pools, awaiting the next high tide that will wash them back out to sea.

Still Waters

Whenever we spend a day at the seashore, my daughter always has the uncanny ability of thrusting her hand into a seemingly uninhabited tidal pool and coming up with a sea critter—a clam, or a rock crab, sometimes a hermit crab holed up inside somebody else's abandoned seashell. She just sees a glimmer. Or her well-trained eye senses a scurry-induced ripple on the surface on the pool. She knows how skittish creatures think and where they hide.

She didn't learn that from a book. She figured it out by watching—silently, patiently. Her brothers and I spent that time scrambling up and down the jetties in the Maine sunshine on those warm summer days. She was content to stare, to study, and to stay focused.

Sometimes, bawdy little boys, far too impatient or restless to catch a crab, benefit from her skill when she pulls a baby crab out of her pail. "Here you go. You can play with Pinchy," she tells one amazed little tyke.

Sometimes we have to wait on God and study a still pool before plunging in. The rewards are great.

The golden shimmer in the eastern sky off the coast of Maine is merely a reflection of the sun's glory as it sets in the west.

Tucked into a safe, calm harbor, boats are protected from fierce Atlantic storms.

On the island of Nantucket, Sankaty Light signals ships as they approach the shoreline.

Lord, may we also reflect your Son's glory, shelter others from the storms of life, and warn those around us of impending dangers.

Disposable

Last week I bought a nice new wallet. And I took all my precious valuables out of my old, worn-out wallet and placed them in the new one. For a moment I considered how over the last seven years I have guarded that old wallet and spent a great deal of mental effort hiding and protecting it, always being conscious of its whereabouts. I have expended much careful thought making sure it was always with me. And then I found myself unceremoniously tossing this most precious object into the garbage. Battered and worn, tattered and torn, that wallet had lost its usefulness, though its contents still had value.

So it is when we die. This worn-out shell that we took so much care of is cast off. The valuable contents, not the "wallet" that protected them, go on into eternal life. Every inspired sermon and every well-written book that encourage us to live a Christian life bear witness to this: when the body dies, Christ-like character is the precious commodity that remains.

Perkins Cove provides a safe harbor for all kinds of boats.

On the Summer Solstice, the sun rises right at 5:00 am in Ogunquit, Maine.

The lobster shacks of Perkins Cove, Maine are sometimes enshrouded in fog.

Sand sculpture contests at Hampton Beach in New Hampshire feature imaginative works of art.

The message of the Cross in sand.

Imaginative sand sculptors create elaborate works of art, knowing that time and tide will soon destroy them.

But if we walk in the light...

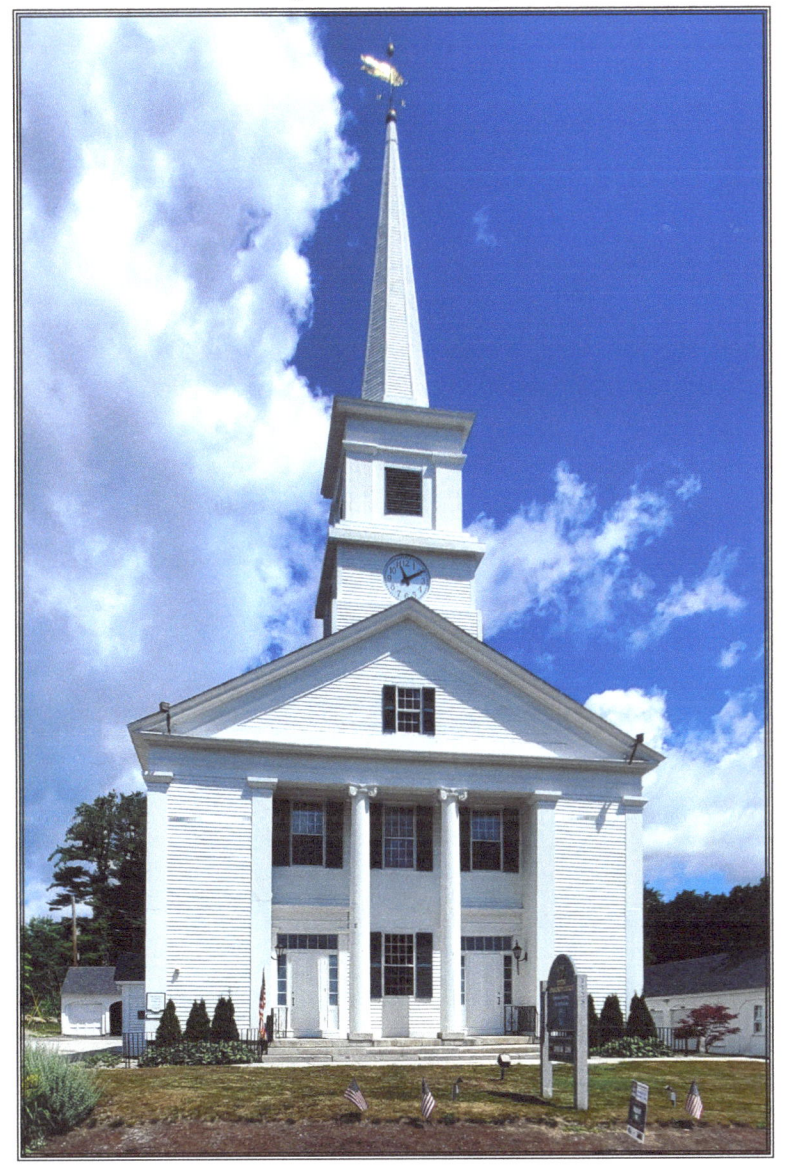

...as he is in the light...

...we have fellowship with one anotehr. (1 John 1:7)

Seen by Heaven

Flower boxes grace many Nantucket homes.

The men of the church often gather for fellowship events. And, as men often do, they speak passionately about their latest exploits in whatever line of work they have been called to do. Not so with Larry, who no longer needs to work outside the home. Instead, Larry spends much of his time in quiet, humble, behind-the-scenes service to fellow church members in need—a delivery, a ride, a prayer—whatever act of kindness is needed. Larry is gainfully unemployed, using his time in acts of service, building a résumé seen by Christ, recorded in heaven.

A walking bridge over the Deerfield River delights those who cross it with beautiful flowers.

The Two Editors Inn in Poultney, Vermont on a summer afternoon.

I will not give sleep to my eyes
or slumber to my eyelids,
until I find a place for the LORD,
a dwelling place for the Mighty One of Jacob. (Psalm 132:4–5)

Jack, Quack, and their six siblings follow mother Duck in the Boston Commons garden.

Well-preserved brick homes line the narrow streets of Beacon Hill.

The 306'-tall Bennington Battle Monument commemorates one of three battles that marked the turning point of the Revolutionary War.

Right Before My Eyes

In Franconia, New Hampshire, one can ride an aerial tram to the top of Cannon Mountain and enjoy the views.

A brilliant summer sun was setting over Vermont's Green Mountain majesty, flinging a splendor of colors across the evening sky. As viewed through my sunglasses, the effect of the colors was even more striking—subdued, shifted slightly, and free of glare. A quick snapshot with my phone's camera recorded a good photo, but I wanted an excellent one. I wanted my camera to capture this moment as seen through my sunglasses.

So, I positioned the sunglasses directly in front of the camera and clicked. To my dismay, the camera refocused itself and took a picture of my sunglasses. I struggled with my phone's camera over and over, trying to get it to understand that it should think of my sunglasses as a filter, an extra lens, a camera attachment. But it insisted that the sunglasses themselves were the object to be photographed.

Exasperated, I had to concede that it was unable to distinguish lens from object. It obsessively kept focusing on what was right in front of it instead of seeing the big picture and just using the sunglasses to color its view of the real object—that glorious sunset. Happily, after much struggling, I did manage to trick it into focusing on the sunset and photographing through the sunglasses.

Sometimes we are so focused on the immediate that we miss the long view. The Lord shows us far-off glories, and we miss them in our obsession over what lies immediately before us. Like the camera, we only focus our energy on the immediate, while missing what lies off in the distance. We focus on earthly things, instead of seeing them in the light of glory.

A trip on the Kancamagus highway takes you through gorgeous mountain views.

What beauty lies in the White Mountains of New Hampshire!

The Connecticut River forms the 160-mile boundary between Vermont and New Hampshire.

Even at small churches in the mountains, people need to hear a clear presentation of the gospel.

What splendor God put into His creation.

Set your minds on things that are above, not on things that are on earth. (Colossians 3:2)

Getting Directions

Using a GPS device in Northern New England can lead an unwitting driver astray. Natives know the roads in their locale well, discerning which ones are navigable in a small passenger car, and which are not. And they understand the limitations that the mud season of late March places on unpaved, rut-filled mountain backroads. A GPS only understands the shortest distance between two points. Occasionally a chagrined flatlander must stop and ask directions from a mountain-born native who often gives terse advice that begins with, "You're not from around here, are you?"

Everyone makes choices in life. Sometimes on that journey, they realize that what they thought was the quickest way to get what they wanted was actually nothing more than a dead-end road. Sometimes the route leads only to disaster. What we really should want is to choose the path that leads to heaven. Sadly, some people never figure out they are on the wrong road and will never get there. Christians grieve when we see people like that. We picture the Lord standing there saying the same thing that the candid, plainspoken New Englander says to the lost traveler: "You can't get there from here."

Near Arlington, Vermont, the interwoven mountains provide an unusual effect.

In some places, the severe rock faces of the White Mountains of New Hampshire resemble those in the Rocky Mountains.

Imaginative teens near Wallingford, Vermont created a table in case giants come for dinner.

Indomitable Spirit

The early settlers from the British Isles found New England—particularly New Hampshire—to have pretty rocky soil. Unlike the lush, fertile soil out near the Great Lakes, New England's ground is full of rocks. Rocks and stones, and more rocks, and more stones.

The settlers were not deterred. They dredged out the rocks and used them. They built foundations, mills, chimneys, porches and walkways out of field stones. And they built rock wall fences.

Originally the overabundance of rocks and stone hampered the settlers' efforts to plant crops. Undaunted, the thrifty, industrious farmers turned the bane of their existence into beautiful rock wall fences. They overcame a barrier by turning it into a protective asset.

In downtown Nantucket, the main street is still paved with cobblestones. Tourists marvel at how charming it looks.

We all face stony problems. But sometimes God gives us grace to turn them into something wonderful.

Perhaps Rocky Obstacles Become Lovely Examples Miraculously.

A handsome church on a hilly road rising up out of Weston, Vermont.

September

September swallows summer's sultry sun-drenched skies,
Allowing the ardent anticipation of autumn's arrival.
First fires in the fireplace find us frolicking in fall's foliage.

Sometimes in prayer the Lord illuminates our situation and we see the beauty of it, even though the sky is gray.

When life gets tedious, the Lord uses the grandeur of His mountains to remind us of His power.

Serenity reigns at a mountain pond near Andover, Vermont.

In their case the god of this world has blinded the minds of the unbelievers,
to keep them from seeing the light of the gospel of the glory of Christ, who is the image
of God. (2 Corinthians 4:4)

A mountain stream in East Arlington, Vermont provides a playful waterfall.

A lone tree keeps watch over an autumn meadow..

Pray that the preachers in all the churches of the region would lead their congregations in biblical truth.

We honor visionary men who pointed out the way and led men courageously.
We need more men like this today.

A mountain stream passes behind quaint old mill buildings in East Arlington, Vermont.

Pumpkins, gourds, and maple syrup—another harvest of good things God has given us to enjoy.

You are the light of the world. A city set on a hill cannot be hidden.
(Matthew 5:14)

Fascinating homes like this one fire the imaginations of children going by them.

Apple cider and fresh donuts are a must during a visit to the Cold Hollow Cider Mill.

Some churches attract people with their unusual designs; pray that all the churches would attract people with effective gospel preaching.

For what does it profit a man to gain the whole world and forfeit his soul? (Mark 8:36)

October

Without the heat of summer's sun, the balmy days have flown.
So now unto the autumn air each leaf must give its own.
The windy nights and chilling frosts across the land now roll.
And so, unto the chilling air each leaf submits its soul.

Bright greens, a lush of foliage, once covered all the hills.
They've laid aside their monotones and yielded to the chills.
Today, for their concessions then, a glory bright and new
   Stands as a testimonial for everyone to view.

A leaf is blessed so greatly here: in giving it receives.
A pity some men reckon not the lesson shown in leaves.
Plain green has turned to brilliant hues: one color now is many.
A blaze of glory spreading out—before there wasn't any.

Today we see our splendored hills, a sight we hold on loan—
   For into God's creative hand each leaf once gave its own.

Back roads provide the best views of maple trees at peak foliage in October.

Red barns and orange leaves make a great combination on an autumn day.

A miniature version of the Park-McCullough mansion in North Bennington, Vermont was once the playhouse of the millionaire's daughter.

A mountain stream passes behind quaint old mill buildings in East Arlington, Vermont.

Only Two Destinies

Maple seeds. Anyone in this corner of the country can tell you that maple trees drop a lot of seeds in the spring. By God's design, each seed comes equipped with its own little "parachute" wing that enables it to spin wildly in the breeze and travel a ways away from the mother tree. Every seed bears the potential of becoming a new, strong, glorious maple tree; each one is carried away by wind to find a home in the welcoming earth. No two seeds, nor their resulting trees, are truly identical.

And then they diverge. A myriad of maple seeds never find a home in the ground. They land on streets and sidewalks and are seen as useless, half-rotted trash to be scornfully raked up and thrown away. But some seeds do land in fertile soil and, after decades of growth, they become strong trees, producing joy, beauty, maple sugar, and stunning foliage to delight the next generation.

Only two destinies are possible: to be cast into perdition, or to grow into something magnificent.

In this simple and profound way, God the creator has shown us the only two destinies of the human soul.

Though the dog was not for sale, the Vermont Country Store features fascinating items from bygone days.

Many rural towns have village squares with gazebos, but few are as lovely as the one in Rochester, Vermont on an autumn day.

A home in Stowe, Vermont, one of the finest ski resorts in New England.

The Henry Covered Bridge: New Englanders covered their bridges to keep them free from snow and ice.

A hand-painted moose shows off classic New England scenes.

We destroy arguments and every lofty opinion raised against the knowledge of God, and take every thought captive to obey Christ.
(2 Corinthians 10:5)

Old Bennington's village green is flanked by marble sidewalks and a picket fence.

If the end of every person is the grave, how should we then live?

The famous poet Robert Frost and his family are buried in the Old Bennington cemetery.

When contrasted with orange leaves and lit by the sun, dull gray clouds take on beauty.

A handsome gazebo graces the center of the village square in Weston.

A river is change—constant flux, never the same for a second, like the spirit of the living God that is always moving in the hearts of men.

Backroading in autumn provides an escape into the handiwork of God's creation.

November Pause

Yesterday the yellow yards of October did astound us
  filled with flaming fall foliage,
  full of flares, a feast for the eyes.
Enjoy, we said, enjoy!

Now the still, silent shroud of November does surround us
  blocked by black, bare branches,
  blustering breezes, and blue-grey skies.
Rest, she tells us, rest.

Soon the frantic, frenzied fun of December will confound us
  with its wet, winter whiteness,
  wind-swept days, and wondering-why's.
So, rest for the moment.
Rest.

The Word of the Lord is living water, carrying us toward peace and truth.

Autumn's chill reveals the beauty inside the leaves.
With God's grace at work, trials reveal Christ's love in us.

Salt is good, but if salt has lost its taste,
how shall its saltiness be restored? (Luke 14:34)

Not Alone

We read to know that we are not alone. When we read, we hear of the struggles, challenges, joys, and victories of others. We relate to their anguish. We rejoice to hear news of victory. To read the words of another, beset with the same foibles and sorrows as we, is to connect into community. The writings of others build bridges between our mortal souls and theirs. In excellently-crafted novels, we identify with a hero or heroine as that person struggles against the world and we ourselves grow and change.

New England has produced great classic writers, from Jonathan Edwards, a genius-level theologian of the 18th century, and celebrated novelists like Nathaniel Hawthorne, to famous hymn writers like Fanny Crosby and Katharine Lee Bates. The writings of these faithful New Englanders have informed and inspired our nation for centuries. Their works are a national treasure.

We write to let others know that they are not alone.

In Hartford, Connecticut one can tour the home of Harriet Beecher Stowe, whose writings affected America so deeply that they sparked a war to end slavery.

John Sergeant lived in the Mission House in Stockbridge, Massachusetts where he brought the gospel to native Americans in that region, as did David Brainerd, whose writings inspired generations of Christians to devote their lives to foreign missions.

Step back into 1914 in this room at the Hogue Library of Northeastern Baptist College, which recreates the look and feel of an old-fashioned New England library room filled with antiquarian books that honor Christian truth.

Christmas Morning Philosophy

A famous philosopher once propounded this conundrum:

"If God is all-powerful, let Him create a rock so large that He cannot lift it."

This has been shown to be ridiculous by the rules of logic because, by definition, omnipotence precludes inability.

However, it is striking to note that only God is so powerful that He could incarnate Himself into the form of a human being who, being born of God, was indeed truly God, and yet also a being of limited scope. Indeed, God IS so powerful that He can create a rock so large that, in the form of a newborn baby, He cannot lift it.

During Advent, Vermont's oldest inn, the Dorset Inn, provides a quintessential Christmastime setting.

Christmas shops offer many things to make the season merry and bright.

Candles of Advent

Candles of Advent, four tapers burning.
Swiftly four weeks fly quickly away.
Lighting our evening, our time of yearning.
Hope, Joy, Light and Love brighten our day.

This baby Jesus, friend to the stranger,
Come as a savior down to the earth.
Babe wrapped in swaddling lies in a manger,
Forsaking glory, humble his birth.

Born of a virgin, hope of the nations
Sent to a scene of stable and stone.
Miracle, mystery, humiliation–
Savior of souls he claims for his own.

O joyous morning! Come, baby Jesus.
All we have sought is granted today.
Be born in us, now. Find us and seize us.
Like these four candles, light up our way.

At Christmas time, churches have a golden opportunity to share the good news of a Savior's birth.

Seek God in Prayer

Churches all across New England need revitalization and an awakened vision of the power of God at work in them. We need to seek God earnestly in prayer that He would send the Holy Spirit's enlivening touch in our day, and that we would be prepared in repentance and humility.

For the LORD your God is testing you...

...to know whether you love the LORD your God...

...with all your heart...

...and with all your soul. (Deut. 13:3)

A new day, a new sunrise, a new light is now on the horizon—let the light of God illuminate His churches.

Closing Thought

We will not hide these things from the children,
but will tell them to the coming generation:
the glorious deeds of the LORD, and his might,
and the wonders that he has done. (Psalm 78:4)

In this psalm we can see our mandate. It is vital that each generation of believers pass on its passion and values and genuine gospel message to the next. For centuries this did happen in New England. But tragically, for the last century, each succeeding generation in New England has strayed farther from biblical truth than the one before it. Now, this region is in dire need of hearing biblical truth preached and responding to the gospel in repentance and belief.

This land of New England holds a unique place in history. It was the birthplace of American Christianity in many significant ways. And, God blessed the people of this region with great spiritual awakenings—the Holy Spirit working in tandem with godly preachers of His Word.

When we pray for this land to be awakened, we pray for a new morning. We ask the Lord to bring the light of truth to a spiritually dark area. We pray that the Holy Spirit would call people to Himself, as He did in the first and second Great Awakenings.

When we pray that revival would begin, we also begin to realize that it must begin with us. As we study the nature of revival, we realize that many of us are not ready for it. And we keep realizing new things like the fact that true revival might "cost" us something. We need to grasp the reality of the revival we are praying for.

So, in both senses of the word we cry:
"O Lord, may it dawn on us."

Locations of Photographs

front cover	York, Me.
title page	Danville, Vt.
p.3	Providence, R.I.
p.4, upper	Bennington, Vt.
p.4, lower	Providence, R.I.
p.5	Old Bennington, Vt.
p.6, upper	Old Bennington, Vt.
p.6, lower	Bennington, Vt.
p.7, upper	Old Bennington, Vt.
p.7, lower left	Bennington, Vt.
p.7, lower right	Old Bennington, Vt.
p.8	Newfane, Vt.
p.9	Old Bennington, Vt.
p.10	Pittsford, Vt.
p.11	Chester, Vt.
p.12, upper	Chester, Vt.
p.12, lower left	Old Bennington, Vt.
p.12, lower right	Nantucket, Mass.
p.13, upper	North Bennington, Vt.
p.13, lower left	Northfield, Mass.
p.13, lower right	Chester, Vt.
p.14, left	Williamstown, Mass.
p.14, right	Collinsville, Conn.
p.15	[not from New England]
p.16, all	Hartford, Conn.
p.17, upper left	Mystic, Conn.
p.17, upper right	York Beach, Me.
p.17, lower left	Vergennes, Vt.
p.17, lower right	Shaftsbury, Vt.
p.18, left	South Windsor, Conn.
p.18, right	Providence, R.I.
p.19, left	Wallingford, Vt.
p.19, upper right	Chester, Vt.
p.19, lower right	Williamstown, Mass.
p.20, left	Dorset Hollow, Vt.
p.20, upper right	Webster, Mass.
p.20, lower right	North Bennington, Vt.
p.21, upper	Quechee, Vt.
p.21, lower	Tyson, Vt.
p.22, left	Perkins Cove, Me.
p.22, upper right	Pemaquid, Me.
p.22, lower right	Cape Elizabeth, Me.
p.23, upper left	Scarborough, Me.
p.23, upper right	Perkins Cove, Me.
p.23, lower left	Ogunquit, Me.
p.23, lower right	Perkins Cove, Me.
p.24, upper	York Beach, Me.
p.24, lower	Portland, Me.
p.25, upper	Perkins Cove, Me.
p.25, lower	Ogunquit, Me.
p.26, upper left	Kennebunkport, Me.
p.26, lower left	Christmas Cove, Me.
p.26, right	on Nantucket Island, Mass.
p.27, left	Ogunquit, Me.
p.27, upper right	Perkins Cove, Me.
p.27, lower right	Perkins Cove, Me.
p.28, all	Hampton Beach, N.H.
p.29, left	Dublin, N.H.
p.29, upper right	York, Me.
p.29, lower right	West Stockbridge, Mass.
p.30, upper	Nantucket, Mass.
p.30, lower left	Shelburne Falls, Mass.
p.30, lower right	Poultney, Vt.
p.31, left	Old Bennington, Vt.
p.31, right	Boston, Mass.
p.32, all	Franconia, N.H.
p.33, upper left	Livermore, N.H.
p.33, upper right	Orville, N.H.
p.33, lower left	Sugar Hill, N.H.
p.33, lower right	Livermore, N.H.
p.34, upper	Arlington, Vt.
p.34, lower	Franconia, N.H.
p.35, upper	Wallingford, Vt.
p.35, lower	Weston, Vt.
p.36, upper right	Jeffersonville, Vt.
p.36, left	Arlington, Vt.
p.36, lower right	Weston, Vt.
p.37, upper left	East Arlington, Vt.
p.37, lower left	North Bennington, Vt.
p.37, right	Woodstock, Vt.
p.38, left	Old Bennington, Vt.
p.38, upper right	East Arlington, Vt.
p.38, lower right	Pownal, Vt.
p.39, upper left	North Bennington, Vt.
p.39, lower left	Stowe, Vt.
p.39, right	Richmond, Vt.
p.40	Sandgate, Vt.
p.41, left	East Arlington, Vt.
p.41, upper right	North Bennington, Vt.
p.41, lower right	North Bennington, Vt.
p.42, left	Rochester, Vt.
p.42, right	Weston, Vt.
p.43, upper left	Stowe, Vt.
p.43, lower left	North Bennington, Vt.
p.41, right	Old Bennington, Vt.
p.44, all	Old Bennington, Vt.
p.45, upper left	Bennington, Vt.
p.45, upper right	Weston, Vt.
p.45, lower left	North Bennington, Vt.
p.45, lower right	Shaftsbury, Vt.
p.46, upper	North Bennington, Vt.
p.46, lower	Arlington, Vt.
p.47, upper left	Hartford, Conn.
p.47, lower left	Stockbridge, Mass.
p.47, lower right	Bennington, Vt.
p.48, left	Dorset, Vt.
p.48, right	Sunderland, Vt.
p.49	Old Bennington, Vt.
p.50, upper left	Enfield, Conn.
p.50, upper right	E. Poultney, Vt.
p.50, lower left	Westmoreland, N.H.
p.50, lower right	North Berwick, Me.
p.51	Old Bennington, Vt.
rear cover	Rochester, Vt.

May the light of the gospel shine brightly, lighting up every church in the region.

About the Author

Jim Mancuso and his wife Kathleen reside in Niskayuna, New York. They are blessed to have three grown children and four wonderful grandchildren. As one of the founding faculty of Northeastern Baptist College in Bennington, Vermont, Jim currently serves as Head Librarian and teaches English. He also serves as an elder of First Presbyterian Church in Schenectady. Jim's other interests include linguistics, Bible translation, seashells, and the history of the Great Awakenings.

All photographs in this album are the original work of Jim Mancuso, taken throughout his ramblings across New England.

www.ingramcontent.com/pod-product-compliance
Lightning Source LLC
Chambersburg PA
CBHW041644220426

43661CB00018B/1291